## How to use this book

*Follow the advice, in italics, given for you on each page.*
*Support the children as they read the text that is shaded in cream.*
**Praise** *the children at every step!*

*Detailed guidance is provided in the Read Write Inc. Phonics Handbook*

## 8 reading activities

*Children:*
- *Practise reading the speed sounds.*
- *Read the green and red words for the story.*
- *Listen as you read the introduction.*
- *Discuss the vocabulary check with you.*
- *Read the story.*
- *Re-read the story and discuss the 'questions to talk about'.*
- *Re-read the story with fluency and expression.*
- *Practise reading the speed words.*

# Speed sounds

**Consonants**  *Say the pure sounds (do not add 'uh').*

| f  | l   | m  | n  | r  | s  | v   | z  | (sh) | th | ng   |
|----|-----|----|----|----|----|-----|----|------|----|------|
| ff | (ll)| mm | nn | rr | ss | (ve)| zz |      |    | (nk) |
|    |     |    | kn |    | ce |     | s  |      |    |      |

| b  | c   | d  | g  | h | j | p  | qu | t    | w    | x | y | ch  |
|----|-----|----|----|---|---|----|----|------|------|---|---|-----|
| bb | k   | dd | gg |   |   | pp |    | (tt) | (wh) |   |   | tch |
|    | (ck)|    |    |   |   |    |    |      |      |   |   |     |

**Vowels**  *Say the sounds in and out of order.*

| at | hen  | in | on | up | day | see   | high | blow |
|----|------|----|----|----|-----|-------|------|------|
|    | head |    |    |    |     | happy |      |      |

| zoo | look | car | for | fair | whirl | shout | boy |
|-----|------|-----|-----|------|-------|-------|-----|

Each box contains one sound but sometimes more than one grapheme. Focus graphemes are **circled**.

## Green words

*Read in Fred Talk (pure sounds).*

w<u>h</u>en   ha<u>ve</u>   bu<u>nk</u>   g<u>row</u>   <u>own</u>   s<u>l</u><u>ee</u>p   <u>sh</u> <u>ee</u>t
c<u>oo</u>l   p<u>oo</u>l

---

*Read in syllables.*

p<u>l</u>ay`r<u>oo</u>m → p<u>l</u>ayr<u>oo</u>m         bed`r<u>oo</u>m → bedr<u>oo</u>m         bo<u>tt</u>`om → bo<u>tt</u>om

co<u>ck</u>`a`t<u>oo</u> → co<u>ck</u>at<u>oo</u>     ka<u>ng</u>`a`r<u>oo</u> → ka<u>ng</u>ar<u>oo</u>     ro<u>ck</u>`et → ro<u>ck</u>et

b<u>ee</u>t`r<u>oo</u>t → b<u>ee</u>tr<u>oo</u>t       mu<u>sh</u>`r<u>oo</u>m → mu<u>sh</u>r<u>oo</u>m     pi<u>ll</u>`<u>ow</u> → pi<u>ll</u> <u>ow</u>

## Red words

be    <u>th</u>ere    my    no    so    a<u>ll</u>

# Vocabulary check

Discuss the meaning (as used in the story) after the children have read each word.

definition:

**bunk beds**   one bed on top of another

**cockatoos**   unusual bird

**cool**   smart

Punctuation to note in this story:

| | |
|---|---|
| When   My | Capital letters that start sentences |
| . | Full stop at the end of each sentence |
| ! | Exclamation mark used to show excitement |
| ... | Wait and see |

# So cool!

*Introduction*
Do you ever dream of having your own place, where you can have your own friends around, eat what you want, do what you want?

Story written by Gill Munton
Illustrated by Tim Archbold

When I grow up, I will get my own flat.

I will have:

- a big playroom

- a bedroom with bunk beds – I will sleep on top and Big Fluff can sleep in *the* bottom bunk

- sheets and pillows with rockets on them

- **no** bathroom

- a big swimming pool

- lots of pets, three dogs and a kangaroo, and six cockatoos on **the** roof

- all the right food – bowls of pasta with cheese and lots of sweets (no beetroot, and no mushrooms)

My flat will be cool.
It will be so cool!
When I grow up ...

# Questions to talk about

Re-read the page. Read the question to the children. Tell them whether it is a **FIND IT** question or **PROVE IT** question.

FIND IT
- ✓ Turn to the page
- ✓ Read the question
- ✓ Find the answer

PROVE IT
- ✓ Turn to the page
- ✓ Read the question
- ✓ Find your evidence
- ✓ Explain why

| Page 9:  | FIND IT  | What does she want to have in her bedroom? |
| Page 10: | FIND IT  | What pets would she keep? |
| Page 12: | FIND IT  | What would she cook? |
| Page 13: | PROVE IT | Do you think she will change her mind when she gets older? |